LIFE IS HARD WITHOUT YOUR SHADOW

UNTOLD

SHUBHAM SINGH

Contents

Contents

1. I Wish I Could

I could have praised thy beauty,
I could have praised thy smile,
I could have praised thy scent,
I could have praised thy name.
I could have praised thy glance,
I could have kissed thy forehead,
And held thee close in mine arms.
I could have—I could have—
Before I lost thee.
I could have praised thy grace,
Thine eyes, thy timeless beauty,
And the life thou bringest.
I wish I could bear
The pain and love
That dwelleth within thee.
I wish I could walk beside thee,
Hand in hand upon thy path.
I wish I could love thee
As he doth—
Yet I remain, longing,
Falling over and over
For thy smile.
For thee, mine lufu,
Lufu and lufu.

I would be both Sātan and Sāenct,
To love thee, to shield thee,
To love thee still.
I wish—I could.

2. Beyond Beauty, Beyond Reason

She is not a rose,
Nor a delicate lily,
Not the fragrance every man desires,
Not the bright sky,
Nor the whisper of mountain winds.
Her breath is not of spring flowers,
Her face carries the marks of time,
Is she beautiful? Perhaps not.
Then why do I love her?
Is she the wisest of all?
Why do I admire her?
She is joy itself,
A light in my hollow soul,
A stream of water in the desert,
The kind of solace every man longs for.

3. Wake Me from the Dream

Slap me,
wake me from this dream—
a dream where I was loved
by you,
so beautiful, so peaceful.
Wake me to reality,
let it hit me hard,
let me feel the sting,
for I am no longer loved
by my queen.
How do I believe
this sudden break,
so quick, so cruel?
It is hard to breathe.
Wake me—
to reality.

4. A Victory in Love

I might have lost,
but still, I have won.
My love—
even without you by my side,
I smile through my tears,
finding joy in my devotion.
For love is not just in having,
but in cherishing,
in honoring the beloved,
no matter the distance.
No matter the love.

5. Goofy Love

I am in Goofy love,
Where stēorras speak to the sun,
And melt,
To shower light upon the night.
Twinkle—
I wish thou be mine Goofy love,
Cherished with lilies and sunflowers,
A sunny day, a sky soft with clouds,
Rains and rainbows.
I wish
To fall for thy smile,
Blessed by thy presence,
And lost in the depths of thine eyes.
I wish to be thy Goofy love,
Like autumn's first breath,
Like the first rain,
And the scent of earth reborn.
I wish to be Goofy,
Goofy, mine lufu,
For thee, mine love.

6. Let me write

The last cry of love,
A last time,
When I loved her,
I talked about her smile,
Her infinite eyes,
Her sweet voice
Let me write
The last cry ,
I never loved her,
And never cared,
I be rude to her,
Even if she cry
I be moved by it,
Shaken, and pain
What I do my love,
Let me write
My last cry,
I have learned to suffer,
And carry blames
It's heavy, I will manage
I will take this one too,
And name it
The last cry

7. A Love That Simply Is

I love her not just for how she makes me feel,
but for who she truly is.
A love that asks for nothing, yet still hopes,
one that finds beauty in her existence,
even when it brings pain.
It is pure, unselfish, deeply poetic—
not bound by touch, but by presence.
Let my words be the hands that hold her,
the quiet proof that she is cherished.
I am here, without expectation, without demand.
True love is not about clinging,
but knowing when to let go—
even if it breaks me,
even if my heart sinks into silence.
If my love is never returned,
I will carry it with grace,
for it lives in my poetry, my art,
in the way I see the world.
Some love stories are not meant to be lived,
but to be felt—deeply, eternally.
Like the ocean embracing the sky,
like a whispered secret in the wind.
If she ever reads these words,
she will know—whether she speaks or not—

that she was loved in a way few ever are.

8. The Essence of My Love

Is it her kindness?

Her beauty?

The way she speaks, moves, or understands the world?

Or is it something deeper—

an unexplainable force that binds me to her?

If love were removed from the equation,

who would she be to me?

Would I still admire her?

Would she still inspire me?

Love feels like devotion, like surrender,

an endless giving of myself

without expectations,

yet with an unshakable hope.

It is about cherishing her smile, her presence,

even if she is never mine

in the way I desire.

9. The Weight of My Love

Do I wish for her to feel the depth of my love,
or do I long for a response?
Love, at its purest, is a gift without expectation,
a silent offering of my heart.
She may never return my love,
yet she will know the depth of my emotions—
my love, my pain, my unwavering devotion.
She is both my greatest joy and my deepest sorrow,
a presence that lingers, irreplaceable.
Mine is a love that asks for nothing,
a rare purity that seeks no reward.
But beyond love, who is she to me?
What makes her special beyond my longing?
What is love to me, truly?
And why does my heart choose her?

10. A Portrait of You

Amazed with thy presence,
You are a beautiful piece of art,
Untied and feathered,
Silky and soft,
Humorous and bold,
Infinite, and beyond.
Shine and bright,
Incomplete without touch of true love,
Never fading, neither yellow,
God could fall prey to thy beauty,
Handsome and humble.

11. A Love I Never Had

I fear losing what was never mine,
Love, trust, and silent betrayal entwined.
Smiling, though the world turns away,
Swallowed by hate, yet longing to stay.
Heavy arms that could have held her tight,
Yet she was never in my sight.
I fear betraying a love unsung,
A melody lost before it begun.
The gentlest wind breaks me apart,
Scattering pieces of a trusting heart.
Though sorrow lingers, my tears stay dry,
For men don't weep—yet still, they die.

12. Too Old to Be Loved

I feel unworthy,
Unloved by both—
God above
And thee, whom I cherish most.
Too old, too undeserving,
Wrapped in unworthiness and cold.
I seek forgiveness,
Yet crave thy warmth.
Am I too old to belong to thee?
Thy love is out of reach,
A distant dream,
An illusion fading in the mist.
Yet mine love remains—
Strong and undeniable,
Even when it is but a shadow,
A silent echo in the wind.
One-sided and forsaken,
I stand with yearning sadness,
A soul rejected,
Yet still hopelessly thine.

13. Am I Too Old for Love?

It is fresh in my memories,
Like summer and spring—
The night beside the sea,
The cold breeze,
Thy warmth,
And the way thou called my name.
It is fresh in my memories,
When I was young,
Full of youth and joy,
Lost in love.
Am I too old to fall for thee again?
Oh, Almighty,
Bless me with courage,
With fearless eyes to weep,
To swallow pain,
On the saddest of nights.
Am I too old to fall for thee again?
My love is still young—
Bold and vibrant,
A rainbow of romance,
A color so bright,
Even the sky would shy.
I would hold thy hand,
And walk through thy life.

Am I too old to be by thy side?
Oh, mine love, forgive me—
I am a sin.
Not loved by God,
Not loved by thee.

14. Oh, My Love

Oh, mine love,
I am happy to see thee in love,
Yet it is both painful—
And beautiful.
But why, oh why,
Dost thou love another?
I see thee smile and blush,
Lost in romance and memories,
Yet sorrow fills mine heart,
For those moments
Are not meant for me.
I love the way thine eyes sparkle,
How they shine so bright—
How they giggle with tears.
I take a deep breath,
Swallowing mine fear—
The fear of losing thee,
The fear of losing love itself.
Oh, mine love,
Thou art so real,
Yet so far away.

15. Why, My Love, Do You Stop Me?

Why, mine love, dost thou stop me,
From falling again and again,
Into thine infinite eyes?
'Tis a war, 'tis a peace—
Like a peacock,
I dance in joy.
Why, mine love, dost thou stop me,
From kissing thine hand,
And holding it for a while?
Let the passage of time drift by,
Whilst thou art by mine side.
Why, mine love, dost thou stop me,
From loving thee?
Am I not worthy?
Is mine love not yet ripe,
Not yet in full bloom,
Not bright enough?
Why, mine love, dost thou stop me,
From embracing thee in mine arms,
And pressing a kiss upon thy brow,
As if thou wert mine alone?

Why, mine love, dost thou stop me,
Each time I reach for thee?
Am I not who I once was?
Or have I become someone unworthy?
Not perfect, yet still—
I would paint thee into mine life.
Why, mine love, dost thou stop me?
Why, mine love, dost thou stop me?

16. Love Me With Your Touch

No man hath ever loved,
A broken leaf,
Nor mended the scars of time.
To the Almighty, I ask—
Why is love tangled,
Twisted with emotions,
Fooled by time,
And altered by pride?
Why, Love?
I tread the path of the lost,
Breathe in the scent of decay,
Trapped—
Unknowing of mine own worth.
Within mine heart, still a battle—
To love her and turn away,
To love and to lose,
To be ensnared in her infinite eyes,
And decay through the ages.
Oh, mine love,
Love me with thy touch—
With thy touch.

17. I Fear My Love Will Cease

I fear mine love will cease.
I fear I shall not love her.
I fear I shall lose her.
I fear she shall be another's.
I fear the thought.
I fear time slipping away.
I fear—if I love her,
To infinity—shall it be enough?
What is love?
Oh, Love, call me by mine name,
Embrace me ere hollowness
Pierces mine heart
And decays mine soul.
I fear mine love will cease.
I fear—I do not love her,
Like another's.

18. Twisted by Wyrd

I have been twisted by wyrd,
Like a cyning,
All seems to fade,
With lufu and wynn.
Thy sceadu I worship,
Like the sea, the stēorra, and the heofon.
Mine lufu, a hwīta blæd,
Ceald and galdor,
Drifting as the breeze,
A bliss of geardagum,
Yet free.
I have been twisted by wyrd,
Like a cyning,
Wishing to die
In thy arms,
Withhold mine last cry.
Crystal efen, diamond bright,
That thou mayest sell
For water beneath
The stēorra and sky.

19. Beyond the Passage of Time

With the passage of time,

We shall grow old.

But shall mine lufu fade?

I dread to lose it all.

There shall be a darkness of light,

And a night heavy with sorrow and weeping,

Where I shall feel naught but thee,

Yet no lufu remains.

How shall I smile,

When thou leavest mine side?

How shall I breathe,

When thou art beyond mine sight?

Helpless, broken, but dust,

Shall I live—or merely linger as a dead soul?

I shall recite thy tale

To countless hosts,

And weep upon thy grave,

Through the endless tide of time,

When thou art no more by mine side.

Mine soul solidifies,

Yet melts ere it shatters.

And I know—thou shalt never return to hold me.

I dare not speak much of mine pain and sorrow,
For I lufu thee still—
And shall do so,
Beyond the passage of time

20. Oh, My Love

I do not know you enough,

To write a song,

To sing a melody.

I do not know you enough,

To love you more.

To me, love

Is not a passing dream,

Not a fleeting romance

That can be torn apart

By a gust of hate,

Or a forceful blow.

I do not know you enough,

To sing beside you,

To sit for endless hours,

Smiling, falling—

Yet, I love, though I know you not enough.

I have fallen, countless times,

Loving you, longing to hold you,

Wishing to keep you in my arms.

Am I in love, or just lost in a dream?

But I love—

And I am in love!

Like a burning mountain,

And a gentle breeze beneath the sun,

Oh, how I whisper—
How can I love you, oh my love,
Oh my love!

• 26 •

21. I Refuse to Die

I wish my feelings would disappear,
And the north wind freeze my heart.
As the voiceless night grasps my breath,
Still, I refuse to die.
To the glory of timeless love,
To her smile and the song,
To her name whispered in the dark,
I refuse to die.
Let me grow old and decay,
Yet still, I write—
Poems to my love.
I wish my pen could glean my heart,
Soaked in love, on white paper and a rose.
I wish my feelings would disappear,
And in the night, I freeze.

22. Beneath the Same Sky

In hollowness and melancholy,
I drink the passage of tīma,
Endless—endless,
Sorrow and joy.
Love—oh, love,
Thou art my fear,
And loss I suffer,
In the garden of rōsan,
In the valley of stān.
I see and whisper—madly,
Is it thee? Is it thee?
I worship the tears,
Which fall in fear,
Of forleosan thee,
And in the bliss of love.
Thou art not by my side,
Thou art not mine,
Yet, I kiss thee in lyfte,
I breathe thy scent,
And hear thy voice.
And I smile in sorrow,
Hollowness and melancholy—
For we stand beneath the same rodor.

23. Let Me Sing a Sang

Let me sing a sang,
For the evening,
As we hold hands in hand,
And walk a mile.
The silence speaks,
Echoing love and grief,
Bound by distance,
Fading in time.
Let me sing a sang,
In the memories of my love,
In the fear of loss,
In the ache of longing.
Why are you not by my side?
Why do you not manifest?
Why do you not hear me?
I speak—
Let me love you,
In the most beautiful way I can.
Through the pain of losing you,
Through the touch of heartbreak,
Let me love you.
And I beg—
Let me love you.
Hello, Holy Hell.

24. How Can I Not Love Her

How can I not love her?
How can I not cherish her?
Through the sun and the moon,
Through the light and the grey.
How can I not love her,
Through the pain behind my smile,
Through the trust in her words,
Through the wisdom of the world?
I am bound by love—
A love for her.
How can I not love her,
When I fear losing her?
A dream,
A love,
Flowing through my blood and bones,
Running deep in my veins.
Let this story remain untold,
Of losing you, my love.
How can I not love?

25. Sīō to No Lufu (May There Be No Love)

I specan the sparrow,
Under s̄teorra and candel,
Blissian.
Mine breath seeketh her,
And kisseth her infinite eagum,
Blissian.
I heareth when she speketh,
A tone so ethereal, so mystic,
Like dreamwoven whispers in the wind.
Gemynd bindeth me,
A captive through Gēomor,
Whilst sorrow whispereth grey upon mine heorte.
Hollow I awaken,
Sīō to no lufu—
For love hath forsaken me.
Let me witan if I lufode thee,
If ever I cossed thine breath,
Dreamed of thee beside me,
Nurtured thee as a cild of mine sawol.
Let me witan if I ever lufode thee,
If mine smile ros mid thine,
E'en when it smote—

E'en when thou wert not by mine side.
Let me witan if I ever lufode thee,
If I heald thee from the world,
Rejoiced in the rēn,
And fand warmth in the ceald,
Willing to feallan, if only for thee.
Take me to mine sleepless niht,
Where I could forðfæran,
In earmas of unrotlicnes,
Cearo-grieved in sorh and cyrten,
For the los and the wite,
To lufu thee eft and eft,
In sleepless nihtas.
When she smileth!
When she smileth!
If I stayed wacor through the niht,
Breathing thine sibb,
Drifting in thine stenc,
Forðfaren a þusend times—by thine side.

26. Let Me Know If I Loved You

Let me know if I loved you,
If ever I kissed your breath,
Dreamed of you beside me,
Nurtured you as a child of my soul.
Let me know if I ever loved you,
If my smile rose with yours,
Even when it hurt—
Even when you were not by my side.
Let me know if I ever loved you,
If I shielded you from the world,
Rejoiced in the rain,
And found warmth in the cold,
Willing to fall, if only for you.
Let me know if I loved you,
If I stayed awake through the night,
Breathing your peace,
Drifting in your scent,
Dying a thousand times—by your side.

27. When She Smileth

Take me to my sleepless night,
Under the heofon and clouds.
I wish I could coss her,
And wish to breathe.
How can I not lufu her,
And smile at her great stille eyes?
All my sorh and grief
Seemeth a hollow,
Unrædan and empty,
When she putteth on a smile.
I could forþfæran a thousand times,
And speak a tale—
A saga unto the blink of her eyes.
I wished to be lufod back,
I wished to be someone special.
I wish to be sælig,
But no one I had with me—
Only gemynd, memories of joy.
Take me to my sleepless night,
Where I could forþfæran,
In arms of melancholy,
Cearu-grieved in sorrow and cry,
For the loss and the wite,
To lufu her again and again,

SHUBHAM SINGH

In sleepless nights.
When she smileth!
When she smileth!

• 35 •

28. Love to Whisper

I love to whisper,
Truth without twist,
And memories,
Unsung, fresh, and warm.
I love to smile,
To steal a glance,
As the ocean moves,
As the wind hums a song,
Soft and slow.
Today, I love to—
Love to.
To fall again,
To feel you near,
Like a dream I refuse to wake from.
Love, can you be true?
With flesh and blood,
With color and light,
To bloom, to grow, to never fade?
I rest beneath a quiet tree,
Counting leaves like fleeting moments,
Smiling,
Knowing love was real—
Even in loss, I believe,
Even if just for a while.

29. A Shop of Love

My house, a little shop,
Step inside, look around—
Love and roses in my wardrobe,
Soft whispers in the air.
Come to my stōw,
A little messy, a little rough,
Petals to walk on,
Candles flickering like distant stars.
I will sing,
Not of dreams, but of truth,
Of my heart, my dark desires,
Hold you close, like a fēond bound to fate.
I be selfish, a sailor,
Diving deep,
Sinking into what they call love.
Oh love, can you be real?
With flesh and breath, with fire and light?
A secret unsold, buried deep—
To the bottom of my heart,
I sink, I sink,
You, my rose.

30. She Is the Rose

She is the rose,
A shoppe of emotions,
The silent presence that filleth
Mine space with meaning.
She is not but one beloved;
She is the reason love doth breathe.
Her womanly essence is woven
Into every thought,
Every desire,
Every whispered dream.
She is the muse,
The yearning,
The reason behind each murmured word.
Love remaineth sacred,
A "secreta unsolde,"
Buried deep within mine heart.
She is mine joy,
Mine sorrow,
Mine muse—
And e'en untold,
And e'en untouched.

31. Before Her Infinite Eyes

I bow before her infinite eyes,
And speak in hushéd tones.
Doth I fear?
Nay, 'tis mine love—
Expressed, yet unsung,
A melody for her,
Sweet and true.
I be a lion unto the world,
Yet soft am I for mine love,
Like caramel—
Melting, warm, and sweet.
For her lashes' gentle flutter,
I smile and fall,
Deeper still, into love's embrace.
How doth I feel?
I crawl, I tremble,
Like a new soul,
Lost and found,
In the boundless depths of her love.

32. A Love That Fadeth Not

With a sour wine,
I doth gulp mine feelings,
And wish thee love—
To find one
Who loveth thee more than I,
Even as I fade to dust.
'Tis a wonder, this ache,
To feel pain and tears alike.
Hail, fair maiden,
Doth I truly love thee,
Or I lied?
Tell me, mine own—
Was it love, or but a whispered lie?
Mine eyes brim with sorrow,
Yet I bow before thy love—
So gentle, so fine.
Hold mine hand, tight and true,
Ere thy beloved taketh thee
From mine sight,
And I must bear silent witness.
A love that doth pass
Through the passage of time.
I believe in fate,
In despair and divinity,

Yet haunted am I
By cruel truths.
Would that I could remain
In a fair dream,
Where thou art mine.

33. A Love Worth a Song

I could whisper to song,
And convince them to sing melody,
Under thy name,
Soft and sweet,
Naughty and humorous,
Humble and roar.
I wish to drizzle,
And tremble,
Like a drunken fool,
And whisper to all lovers,
And heartbreak,
Fall in love,
One more, last time,
With my beloved's beauty,
Elegant and graceful.
I could decorate,
Christmas with light in summer,
And sing fairy folk,
Lyrics from my love,
To envy all lovers,
Who loved,
Who loved!

34. Forever in My Heart

You are always on my mind,
As I sit to write,
You flow through my pen,
Bringing light into my world.
How lucky I am to have you by my side.
Your smile stays with me,
Your laughter—music I never forget.
Every moment we share feels precious.
I can't wait to see you again,
To create more memories,
To hold your hand a little longer,
To lose myself in your eyes.
My fingers run through your hair,
A kiss on your forehead, soft and true.
I embrace you, breathe you in,
As if you are the very air I need.
I fall into the moment,
Hoping it never fades,
Keeping you close—
Forever in my heart.

35. Breath of You

To me, breath holds—
Beneath your eyes,
And smiles above the sky.
I breathe—blessed,
When you are by my side.
I desire to hold it,
Deep within my heart,
In memories and smiles,
Of you, forever.
Your presence feels like petals & flowers,
A fragrance that lingers when you pass by.
The breeze in your breath,
A whisper against my soul.
I could hold my breath,
And let it sink within me,
A spring to new life,
Full of joy, full of you.

36. Love That Changed Me

My love is not like

A spark at first sight,

But a fire shaped by time—

Complicated, deep, enduring.

It has changed me,

Turned my worst to good,

Made me admire the man I've become.

I love not to lie,

So trust me, my love,

I have been true.

Have I ever loved you?

Or do I still?

I have bowed before your eyes,

Adapted to your world,

Yet, no matter the future,

I seek pardon—

For I am a wanderer,

A piece of art,

And you, the only craftsman

Who could shape my love,

Yet left it untouched, unwelcome.

It is hard not to break.

I stand strong before the world,

Yet before you, I remain a child—

Unpolished, rough,
Awaiting your touch
To accept my existence,
And love me for life.

37. Love Beyond Time

Do not love me now,
when youth is your glow,
when the world turns to you,
drawn by beauty's fleeting show.
When laughter surrounds you,
when love is abundant,
when admiration fills your days.
Come to me when time has passed,
when beauty fades,
when the world no longer looks your way,
when grace no longer clings to you.
I will take you on a journey,
through stories and memories,
ones I cherished,
ones I dreamed of,
not for the way you looked,
but for the soul beneath.
I have seen beauty more radiant than yours,
faces that mesmerized,
that lured hearts into the trap of desire,
where love was but an illusion,
and lust was the only truth.
But tell me, do I desire you so?
Or is my love a lie?

Come to me when age has touched you,
when time has stripped away the illusion.
I will hold you then,
and love you still—
as though you were 25.

38. A Curse Called Love

O heart, listen to me,
stop breathing through my lungs,
quiet the storm in my mind,
let the tears sink into my bones.
Why do you throw me into love?
I hate you for this burden,
for loneliness that lingers,
for sorrow running through my veins.
There is no melody in this love,
no songs of praise,
only the bitterness of memories,
swallowed like a burning drink.
I wander, lost and restless,
trapped in the vastness of solitude,
a curse both cruel and divine—
to love, and bear its weight.

39. Before I Turn Blind

Before darkness claims my sight,
I wonder how to behold thy beauty—
Under candle's flicker, under golden hues,
To see how sunlight kisses thy lips,
And wakes thee with a smile.
Before I turn blind,
I long to see love in thine eyes,
Unfiltered, radiant, true.
To spend each waking hour reading thee,
Tracing the poetry etched in thy soul.
A restless night,
I shall rise to fight—
Before my world fades to black,
I will wander in memories,
Day and night,
To see thee once more, through the eyes of my past.
Will love fade, if sight is lost?
Nay, my love—
I shall worship thee still,
Carving thy image in the depths of my mind,
And lay to rest my wish to never part.

40. Love Unclaimed

I shall not stand by thee on summer days,
I shall let go thy hand—to let thee rejoice,
To cheat thee, only to see thy smile,
And the tears that follow.
Yet I swear, mine own love is wrought of truth.
Love, I shall return when the nights turn cold,
When storms rage and thunder shatters the sky,
I shall be there, holding thy hand.
I shall wander through youth and beauty untouched,
Yet in mine own heart, thy name shall remain,
Etched in ink, a chapter in mine own book—
Where love sings only for thee.
And when thy tears fall, breaking my truth,
I shall leave thee in summer,
To watch thee dance in joy,
Without fear of being unloved.
Mine own love seeks not thy shadow,
Nor does it wane with time.
It burns unclaimed—like an eternal fire,
A sun that shall never set.
And I, thy Romeo,
A falcon soaring through love's endless story.

41. A Love Song for Eternity

In mine own love song,
I shall weave thy memories,
A melody so deep, so sorrowful,
That every man ever born
Shall weep and mourn in solitude,
Imagining the ache of losing thee.
Yet, I shall ne'er lay blame upon thee,
For is it not beautiful,
When love remains unfinished?
A song sung, a song broken,
Echoing through hearts yet to be born.
With each breath,
Mortal men shall hear our tale,
A love untouched by time.
I shall sit alone, friendless,
Yet smile, as dust takes flight,
Carrying thy name, thy memory—
To eternity.

42. The Last Cry of Lufu

The last cry of lufu,
I mourn in soliloquy,
Wiping mine tears,
And hollowness of forloren.
Breath I cannot hold,
And fyr beneath.
How doth lufu wound so?
How can lufu be forloren?
How canst thou not be?
Be by mine end?
I wish for thy smyl,
And thee by mine side?
I dred!
Hell, I dred!
I mourn in soliloquy,
Wiping mine tears,
In sorrow,
To the last cry.

43. Before I Lose You Forever

Allow me to whisper mine pain into thine ears,
And weep upon thy shoulder.
Allow me—
Allow me to love thee one last time,
Before the sky falleth,
And crusheth mine soul.
Before thou leavest,
I shall be the last leaf,
Dry and yellow,
On the verge of falling.
Hold me, mine love,
Hold me for a while,
Before I break apart,
And lose thee—forever.
And mine tears—
I shall hold them in, for eternity,
Before thy smile,
Before thy smile.

44. Will You Marry Me?

At night, when I hold thy hand,
A melody sings inside my mind—
"Will you marry me?"
Tie me to the thread divine,
Walk with me around sacred fire,
Promise me—never to tire.
Never leave, till my last breath,
I vow, my love will outlast death.
Yet if fate must take its toll,
Let me go first, heart and soul.
With the fall of a rose, soft and bright,
Planted for love, blooming in light.
A love that time shall never sever,
Bound to thee, forever and ever.

45. A Prayer to Be Forgotten

Thou shalt remain in mine eyes,
And I, in mine own words.
Whomever I speak to,
Thy name lingers, unbidden.
'Tis not easy to justify,
Nor to utter what I feel,
For mine heart doth ache deep,
No comfort can soothe—
Save thy touch.
Memories of thee do haunt me,
A torment sweet and cruel.
Love and hell entwined,
A curse I dare not break.
I pray to be forgotten,
To vanish from thy thoughts—
As though we never met.
Oh, Lord, shower me with mercy,
Erase mine existence,
Melt me like ice with time,
Till I rise unseen,
And meet my love in the air.
Let me be her breath,
A whisper upon her lips,
So close—

Yet never known.
I pray,
I pray.

46. Ashamed to Be a Lover

In the eyes of my love,
I am but a shadow of shame,
A regret that lingers,
Flowing through the cracks of time.
How come, my fate?
How come, my heart?
To stand as a lover,
Yet hold no love in return,
No favor, no warmth—
Only an aching soul,
Drenched in the silence
Of a trembling night.
I cry—
Why does love not reach my heart?
Why does fate mock my longing?
I am ashamed to be a lover,
A lover whose faith
Was betrayed by love itself.

47. I Will Walk Away

I will drop you at your destiny,
And I shall walk away,
Without a whisper,
Without a glance back,
Shattering a thousand echoes
Of what we once were.
Do not love me,
Not as I have loved you.
For my love is a chant,
An unbroken hymn,
Etched forever by your name.
Our story shall be sung,
A song of truth,
A melody of longing,
Carved deep within my heart.
I will always be by your side,
Yet unseen, unheard—
A silent shadow in your light.
I will drop you at your destiny,
And I shall walk away.
That is how my love shall bloom—
Unchanged, untouched,
Spine-chilling and eternal.

Oh, my love,
Live—live with my love.

48. Love That Won't Age

Yes, I am here for you,
Night and day,
Like no one else could be.
Praised by millions,
Loved by thousands—
But do I love you like them?
No, dear, I am worse.
I do not love alike,
I hate you instead—
Hate your beauty,
Hate your smile,
Hate your soul,
Hate your eyes.
Mine is a love of hatred.
They will love your body,
They will love your curves,
But do they love you?
Or just the youth that fades?
How long will their love last?
You will be prey
To selfish sellers of affection,
And you will find joy—for a time.
But my love will not age.
It will mirror time,

Etched like a memory of you,
Where my truth remains—
In the void.

49. The Last Night I Write

I remember it be the last night,
When I wrote in mine stories,
And embraced thee in mine words,
Through thy beauty.
How can I forget?
Thy smile,
Thine eyes,
Thy scent—woven in memory.
I remember it be the last night,
When I wrote in mine stories,
To sorrow and pain,
Through melancholy rhythms,
Sung through silence,
Echoed through the night.
I remember it be the last night,
When I wrote in mine stories,
When thou sat by mine side,
And I whispered, "I love thee,"
With mine Goofy smile.
A desert it seems without thee,
Vacant within, hollow.
And I breathe,
For the last time I write.

50. Thee Write

नहीं पूछा तूने

नहीं पूछा तूने, नहीं पूछूँ मैं

    नहीं पूछा तूने, नहीं पूछूँ मैं,

क्यों साथ चल दिए,

वक़्त का कोई पता नहीं,

जो हाथ मलि गया।

    दूरियाँ थीं बड़ी, फिर भी क्यों दिल मिल गया,

दूरियाँ थीं, फिर भी क्यों दिल मिल गया।

नहीं पूछा क्यों, नहीं पूछूँ मैं,

जो साथ चल दिए।

    न वक़्त का पता,

न रास्तों की खबर,

फिर भी कदम बढ़ते रहे,

फिर भी दिल जुड़ते रहे।

    क्यों नहीं पूछा तूने

क्यों नहीं पूछा मैंने?

End Doesn't Matter, it is the Journey